SCHIRMER'S LIBRARY OF MUSICAL CLASSICS

WOLFGANG AMADEUS MOZART

Concertos

For the Piano

Critically Revised, Fingered, and
the Orchestral Accompaniments
Arranged for a Second Piano

G. SCHIRMER, Inc.

DISTRIBUTED BY
HAL•LEONARD®
CORPORATION
7777 W. BLUEMOUND RD. P.O. BOX 13819 MILWAUKEE, WI 53213

Concerto in C Major
for Piano and Orchestra
[K. 415]

Edited by
Isidor Philipp

Wolfgang Amadeus Mozart
(1756-1791)

Cadenza by Mozart